The Pavement Arena

Adapting Combat Martial Arts to the Street

Geoff Thompson

SUMMERSDALE

Summersdale Publishers Ltd
46 West Street
Chichester
West Sussex
PO19 1RP
United Kingdom

www.summersdale.com

Printed and bound in Great Britain.

ISBN 1 84024 184 5

First edit by Kerry Thompson.

Photographs by David W. Monks, member of the Master Photographers' Association
Snappy Snaps Portrait Studio
7 Cross Cheaping
Coventry
CV1 1HF

Important note

If you have or believe you may have a medical condition the techniques outlined in this book should not be attempted without first consulting your doctor. Some of the techniques in this book require a high level of fitness and suppleness and should not be attempted by someone lacking such fitness. The author and the publishers cannot accept any responsibility for any proceedings or prosecutions brought or instituted against any person or body as a result of the use or misuse of any techniques described in this book or any loss, injury or damage caused thereby.

About the author

Geoff Thompson has written over 20 books and is known worldwide for his bestselling autobiography, *Watch My Back*, about his nine years working as a nightclub doorman. He currently has a quarter of a million books in print. He holds the rank of 6th Dan black belt in Japanese karate, 1st Dan in judo and is also qualified to senior instructor level in various other forms of wrestling and martial arts. He has several scripts for stage and screen in development with Destiny Films.

He has published articles for *GQ* magazine, and has also been featured in *FHM*, *Maxim*, *Arena*, *Front* and *Loaded* magazines, and has appeared many times on mainstream television.

Geoff is currently a contributing editor for *Men's Fitness* magazine.

For a free colour brochure of Geoff Thompson's books and videos please ring the 24-hour hotline on 02476 431100 or write to:

Geoff Thompson Ltd
PO Box 307
Coventry
CV3 2YP

www.geoffthompson.com
www.summersdale.com

To my beautiful Sharon

Contents

Introduction

Thirty years ago karate (and all martial arts for that matter) was veiled by a curtain of mystique. If you practised it as an art form, for exercise or purely as a means of self-defence, it went without saying that this mystique extended itself to you, automatically making you a dangerous person in the eyes of others. Competence in self-defence was of course an inevitable by-product, or at least everyone thought so. Talk of registering one's hands with the police as 'dangerous weapons' was commonplace and known karateka were given an extremely wide berth by would-be antagonists.

The aura of mystery surrounding the martial arts grew because there was only a small nucleus of people involved, and it was believed that one was special if a part of that minority. In reality one was not so much 'special' as lucky to find a club or instructor to teach you, as there were so very few of either at that time.

The cinema soon put a stop to that!

With the emergence of Bruce Lee and celluloid kung fu the many-splendoured world of martial arts exploded into our lives with an impressive bang, via posters, film, TV and magazines; vignettes of superhuman fighting, fantastic stories of human endurance and seemingly impossible feats of strength and speed became common. Black belts came out of every crack and crevice in the woodwork, started up clubs, made fortunes and spawned more black belts, who in their turn started up more clubs making more fortunes and more black belts. All of a sudden everyone and their dog was a black belt – or at least they wore one. Due to this popularity and the poor standard displayed by many of the new breed of martial artists, the words 'black belt' lost their magic, and respect for the martial arts declined quickly.

Not long after the celluloid explosion came competition karate. With a multitude of people practising karate and with the emergence of so many new styles and associations, competition became a way in which exponents could fight in a controlled environment, testing their metal against one another in an attempt to discover which of the many contenders would emerge as a champion.

The Pavement Arena

Practising technique in a controlled environment is a good idea, though attempting to find a supreme karate champion isn't.

In their bid to inflate already engorged egos, win yet another competition, and obtain more trophies, fighters began to drift away from the origins of karate in search of tournament techniques and moves that would catch the referee's eye. In many quarters point scoring relegated the martial arts from superb to superfluous, from art to arty, from power to flower power, from hard to lard and from maim to game.

We had become a sport.

Many people did not or could not see this degeneration, believing that competition fighting was the real thing.

In reality of course, street and competition fighting are completely different arenas. Originally the contests did start in the right vein, they were tough, uncompromising arenas where bloody battles were fought and fighting spirit was tested to capacity. Because of this blood and snot element, rules were changed and certain dangerous blows were banned. Controlled technique became the order of the day.

The new rulings shackled many of the warhorses of yesteryear and opened the doors to the wimp element who manipulated and engineered the rule book in their bid to win. Karate was pushed into the world of sport where it lay precariously, like a six-gun in a children's nursery.

The dive became commonplace, and in many cases instinctive. Some team coaches could be heard telling their fighters to stay down so the team might win the bout through disqualification. Every arena around the country, nay the world, had at least one mat that sported fighters performing their renditions of dying flies. Many fighters of the old school pulled away from these new competitions in disgust and entered the full contact ring, joining or forming organisations that embraced the old values. They are as strong and enduring as the roots of an old oak. The wimp element come and go like the seasons, finding nothing of any real substance to hold them and no joy when they throw plastic techniques into the mincer of a live situation only to find themselves beaten into submission.

The Pavement Arena

Nowadays comments on or about karateka are a complete contrast to the compliments of yesteryear. It is common to hear 'He's a good karate man, I wonder if he's any good in the street?'

Karate, in general, is not practised with reality in mind. For this reason many karateka would be ineffective in the street.

Adapted karate is a popular talking point in today's martial arts magazines. Articles about practical street skills are generating far more interest and page space. Why? Because people want and need the skills necessary to take them from the dojo to the street.

A change of ryu is not necessary. Although certain elements within the school may need alteration, it is a change of perception and attitude that is called for. Complacency must be erased and adversity sought if realistic fighting skills are to be attained and retained. It is attitude not aptitude that determines altitude.

In my books *Watch My Back* and *Dead or Alive* I talked about adaptation, though it was outside the scope of both to expand on the matter. This book is dedicated entirely to karate's adaptation. Those who are conscientious enough to adhere to it will surely find improvement and success in the pavement arena.

The Pavement Arena is a book for the practising martial artist, dealing, as formerly stated, entirely with adapting dojo technique to the live scenario. It is not, nor should it be mistaken for a self-defence book, nor is it all encompassing. Adapted karate is, and should be, only 5 per cent of your whole training. The true goal of all martial arts is to bring enlightenment to its practitioners, teaching them humility and respect above all else.

The great Don Draeger once said that we should be so good at our art, so proficient, that if we find ourselves in a room full of people those people should be better protected because of our presence. Not just because we can protect them against the malevolent minority, which of course we can, or at least should be able to do, but also because they are protected against us. Through the adversity of real training in martial arts we should have developed the ability to control ourselves to the degree that we can let people off if they make an error in judgement and insult us. In the higher echelons of the martial arts our concern is less about self-defence and more about self-control. Do you feel confident enough in your art and technique to be able to let people off? Can you control yourself in the car when someone cuts you off and indicates that he thinks you are a wanker? Or do you still find yourself beating up the man on the street because of an insult or a dirty look? Are you perhaps on the other side of the fence where the thought of a real encounter leaves you filled with uncontrollable fear?

My aim with this book is not to try and change the world or start a new style, slag anyone off or even to place myself on a podium. All I want to do is try and offer empirical information to those with an open mind. Proper information, the stuff that might save your life one night when it kicks off outside the chip-shop with a local bully.

Chapter One

Addition and Subtraction

A house is only as strong as its foundations; if the base is weak eventually the house will crumble and fall. So it is with karate. A good solid foundation in basic techniques is very important. Deep stances, repetition of technique, set partner work and kata are all crucial in the building of a strong mind and body, but only if they are practised correctly.

In the following chapters I shall expand more on each individual aspect.

Preparing karate for the street is not only about subtraction, as many believe, subtracting all that is useless until you are left with only that which is useful, but also addition, adding more knowledge and techniques to a syllabus that is lacking.

Everything that is within the karate syllabus should be retained. All of it, in one way or another, has something positive to offer. Even if it appears irrelevant every movement, be it small or elongated, has a meaning and a purpose. Boxers

The Pavement Arena

do not just box, ice skaters do not just skate and actors do not just appear on the stage.

All without exception practise different preparatory exercises. The boxer will, amongst many other things, skip rope, the skater will take ballet classes and the actor will practise voice exercises. Whilst superficially these rehearsals may appear to bear little relation to the finished product, they are still crucial for complete mental and physical preparation.

Knowing why each movement is important, understanding its benefits and relationship to self-defence will help markedly in your development. You are far more likely to perform a technique or exercise correctly if you know the benefits to be had from doing so.

While elongated and exaggerated techniques are a necessary part of karate training to build a strong body and mind, raw technique, that is technique stripped of anything superfluous, elongated or exaggerated, is equally as necessary if the same technique is to be effective in a real situation. The latter should be devoid of anything time-consuming, it must be facile and powered by aggression if it is to be effective. Basically it is a stripped-down version of the dojo technique.

It is important to add to your syllabus anything that you feel it lacks. Generally, with karate, this is hooking punches and grappling movements, both of which can be found in kata. This is one of the reasons why kata practice is so important. To find the hidden movements you must understand the bunkai (application) and this understanding will only come with much practice. Visits to other dojo of different ryu can be very beneficial when looking for new techniques.

The greatest addition you can make, one that seems to be lacking in so many dojos, is attitude; lack of it will see your practice relegated to play. Whether you are punching into the air or practising partner work, instil a 'my life may depend on this technique' attitude into it. When facing a partner in set sparring do not aim your attack to miss, like so many people do, aim to hit, every time. Doing so will generate fear in your partner, then in you when he or she returns the attack with added vigour. This approach will test the metal of the most ardent karateka bringing both of you closer to the 'real thing'. Constant exposure to the fear generated in this way will teach the recipients how to control fear, which, if left unchallenged, might leave them frozen in the face of real danger.

I shall expand more on these points in the relevant chapters.

Chapter Two

Stance

Deep front stance

The Pavement Arena

"The problem with deep stances is that they're not practical!"

How many times have you heard that one? I'll tell you what the problem is, and it's not that deep stances are impractical for the street, but a lack of communication between student and instructor. It is the instructor's responsibility to inform their students what is and isn't practical, and what the technique's function is. Many students, especially of traditional styles, are afraid to ask their sensei about the theory behind a given movement. "Is it practical? Why is it so low?" and so on. Possibly the sensei doesn't know the answers to these questions and in turn was too afraid to ask his or her own sensei. If as an instructor you do not know the answers to the questions that your students pose, be big enough to admit your lack of knowledge and then find the answer from your own instructor. This way the buck stops with you.

This is one of the reasons that so many high Dan karateka are unsuccessful in street scenarios. They attempt to employ techniques that are not adapted for the street and that perhaps need a little tailoring.

Be politely respectful and ask questions as you learn new techniques. If your sensei cannot answer your questions and makes no attempt to find solutions from other sources, get yourself another instructor.

Low stances are not directly practical for a street scenario. They inhibit fast movement and bring you lower in height than your adversary, generally presenting your head as an easy target. However as holding low stances can be excruciatingly painful they are excellent for building powerful leg muscles, endurance and will power. All three, especially the latter, are important pieces of the self-defence jigsaw. Low stances also promote suppleness in the leg muscles contributing greatly to kicking technique.

The accompanying photographs illustrate the short front stance and two traditional stances. Street stances are so stripped-down that you can hardly recognise them.

Short or condensed street front stance

As you can see stance adaptation is merely a case of tailoring them to fit the environment. There are of course many more stances than those illustrated above, but they bear little or no relation to practicality in the pavement arena. For this reason they are not included here, although this is not to say they should not be employed in the dojo where they develop certain qualities. Wherever possible in the street scenario opt for the condensed front stance for best effect as it offers solidity and manoeuvrability.

The high front stance affords accessibility to low kicking techniques and face punches, without impairing balance.

Short front stance

Traditional horse stance

Traditional back stance

Chapter Three

Kicks

When the time and distance are suitable, kicking techniques can be invaluable. Unfortunately, a favourable range for this type of technique is a rarity, and I can see little point in manufacturing kicking distance when other attacking techniques are already immediately available. If you do employ a kick keep it low and sharp as a grabbed foot equals grappling distance, possibly defeat, and at the very least a hard-fought, delayed victory.

It appears that every book that I write sees me insulting the kicker. This is not intentional. Kicking is a highly skilful art, but it doesn't take a M.E.N.S.A. membership to realise that two feet on the ground are more stable and mobile than one. Remember, a slip can end in your defeat; the gratuitously violent minority don't follow Queensberry Rules. If they put you down they will do everything within their power to keep you down. There is nothing to gain and everything to lose by taking risks. I spent the first ten years of my martial arts training learning to kick, and I am a good kicker, only to find that when the pavement was my arena, my kicks fell short of adequate. Sometimes a situation has you so scared that you daren't even move your feet, let alone pick them off the floor to kick with them. Ian, one of my karate friends and a fellow doorman, is an international karateka, and one of the best kickers you could ever meet. This man can really kick. He got into a match fight one night outside a club with a right nutcase, and Ian said he was so scared that at one point in the fight his legs actually collapsed underneath him. Kick? Yes he did kick, but only when his attacker was lying on his back on the floor after Ian had head-butted him. Your feet are important, they allow you to run away when the option is offered and they give you a solid platform for safer techniques, like punching and butting. Remember, just because it works in the dojo that doesn't mean it will work in the street. They are entirely different arenas. Fear changes everything.

It is still important, however, to learn and practise kicking techniques because when the circumstances are favourable and kicks are called for, nothing else will adequately suffice.

As I see it the biggest problem with the traditionally taught kick is its slow retraction after connection with the target, especially the contest-type kick that lingers on contact long enough to show the referee the scored point. In the dojo as well the kick is recovered far too slowly, sometimes the kicker even pivots on the supporting leg for several seconds before its retraction. The reason for this laxness? In the controlled arena there is no penalty imposed on the lazy kicker. A slowly retracted kick in a live situation will be heavily penalised by a leg-grabbing or forward-moving opponent who forces the kicker over. Once you are off your feet the fight changes dimension. A good fighter will never let you stand up again once you are on the ground.

Don't pivot on one leg after kicking.

**High kickers are easily and
frequently pushed over mid-kick**

In chapter eight, 'Sparring', I shall demonstrate the most effective way in which to penalise the lazy kicker to teach him sharper retraction.

To practise fast retraction have a partner try to catch your kicking leg every time you kick. If no partner is available use visualisation to imagine somebody trying to catch your leg. This will encourage correct kick retraction.

Practise trying to catch the kicking leg as your opponent kicks

The Pavement Arena

Alternatively, slowly fully extend your chosen kick into the air, then sharply retract it, placing it on the floor in front of you. Repeat the exercise for as many repetitions as you can before it is uncomfortable, each time trying to pull the kick back a little quicker.

High kicks aimed at face height impair the balance markedly. On an uneven or slippery surface this could prove to be very dangerous leaving the kicker at the mercy of his opponent. If you fall in the dojo your opponent will let you, even help you up. In the street such an error could prove to be your coup de grace, therefore high kicking in a real situation is not recommended. This is not to say that high kicks do not work, only that the risk factor is very high and the penalty for a mistake even higher.

Mid-section kicks, a far safer bet

Mid-section kicks, body shots, are a safer bet, though a kick that is thrust or slowly retracted will be easily caught. Sharp retraction is therefore imperative. The upper abdomen is very well-protected by muscles and is not particularly vulnerable.

Kicks are at their best when aimed 'below the belt'

The lower abdomen below the hip-line is very susceptible to attack, with little muscular protection and easy accessibility. The pubic bone, genitals, thighs, knees and shins are choice targets. Because of the popularity of high kicking however, lower targets are often ignored, so vigilant practice is essential to build your repertoire of techniques.

Anyone familiar with kicks is aware that there are long kicks and there are short kicks. Short kicks lack hip commitment and are used for sharp jabs as opposed to power, though a certain amount of power is still attainable. They bring the kicker too close to the target, often within punching range, making it probable that the attacking foot will either be caught or the kicker punched. They also lead to the unwanted restriction of grappling range, especially the short roundhouse kick. In the dojo where grappling may not be permitted, the effectiveness of the short kick often goes unchallenged, leaving the kicker with a false sense of security. On the street you will be grabbed without hesitation.

It is for this reason that I recommend the more powerful and distanced long kick. The greatest attribute of the long kick is that it keeps your kicking where it ought to be, well clear of the grappler or puncher. Full hip extension will ensure that your kick keeps you at a distance outside your opponent's punching range, and is also the prime source of kicking power.

The following photographs illustrate both the long and the short kick.

Short roundhouse. Sharp but lacks power and distance

Long roundhouse. Note the extra reach obtained by twisting the supporting foot.

Short or close side kick

Long side kick using full hip extension

Front kick

You may employ the ball, heel or instep of your foot to strike your target. Hip thrust behind the kick will ensure power and, if needed, distance. In shoes you should attack using the toe of the shoe.

Roundhouse kick

Strike your target with the ball or instep of your foot. Again, if you are wearing shoes, strike with the toe. For best effect, power and distance, extend the hip (see illustration).

Back kick

A powerful kick, however it requires a high level of skill, especially when executing a spinning back kick. Besides the obvious blind second when your back is turned to your target, as with all spinning kicks disorientation often occurs.

Ready stance

The Pavement Arena

Pivot

Back kick. Powerful but advanced.

It takes highly skilled practitioners to successfully administer back kicks in live situations without placing themselves in grave danger. Danger and skill factor levels are substantially lower if the same kick is employed without the spin, perhaps against an opponent who is directly behind, as opposed to in front of you. It then becomes very basic and effective executed in donkey kick fashion. Fast retraction is again important (see illustration).

When the opponent is directly behind you

The back kick is far more accessible and less advanced

The Pavement Arena

Although the axe kick is a devastating finisher, the stamp kick is quicker and often more efficient than the axe. Lift only the knee and stamp. This is a highly dangerous technique, used in the Second World War as a killing blow. It is pictured here for demonstration purposes and is only recommended if you feel that your life is threatened.

Lift . . .

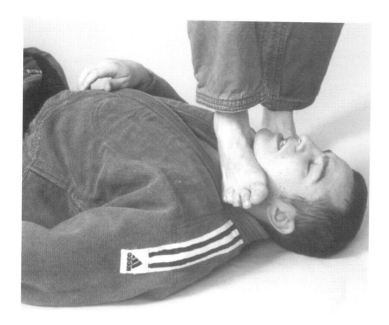

. . . and stamp

Back roundhouse kick

Lacks both power and realism. It is more suited to the contest mat and is not recommended for the street. Its high risk-factor and lack of power make it too dangerous to be considered.

Spinning back roundhouse kick

Though this is a very powerful kick, it also requires a high level of skill. This, along with its low accessibility factor make it unsafe for the street.

Summary

Only employ kicks if the situation demands it. Kick low and recover fast. Wherever possible stick to front, roundhouse, and stamp kicks for best effect. For realism try practising in street clothes and shoes.

Chapter Four

Punches

I spent twelve years doing karate before I admitted to myself that my punching ability and the punching techniques I was being taught in the dojo were too basic.

Front arm   **Reverse punch**

The Pavement Arena

Front arm and reverse punch were all that a very limited curriculum offered – I don't class back-fist strikes as punches. Initially I thought this was enough, after all, I did have my feet as well. How naive I was. Enlightenment came somewhat brutally when I began work as a nightclub doorman, trying to control life's gratuitously violent minority. It was in this environment that I discovered the reality of fighting in an arena that did not shackle its gladiators with rules and regulations; the only rule that your aggressors adhered to was 'there are no rules'. The fighting was frenzied, scrappy and . . . close! Fuck, it was close. Far too close to use the kicks that I'd favoured for so long. Even long range punching found little favour here.

Short range punching, fighting and grappling were the order of the day, and not only because of the tight confines of the pubs. Often the trouble spewed out onto the more spacious pavement, where kicking distance was available, but only for a fleeting moment before it was reduced by an attacking foe who knew only that he wanted to 'get into you' as quickly as possible. In this arena, if you couldn't punch you couldn't fight.

In my search for better coaching I joined the local boxing club under the auspices of Dennis Young, a national ABA (Amateur Boxing Association) coach who acted as my guide through the mechanics of boxing. Every day for a year I was taught privately by a close friend, Mick Finny, also a boxing coach, who kindly gave up his dinner hour in the engineering factory that employed us to add to my education in the field of pugilism. After two seasons in the Cov' Boys where I diligently skipped rope, punched bag and sparred, I attended a four day ABA assistant boxing coach course.

The boxing training and the coaching course opened my eyes and showed me what real punching was all about. I took this new knowledge back to my own students and passed it on so that they might be more prepared for the street than I had been. Ironically I discovered the same boxing-type punches hidden within the karate kata. In chapter six, 'Kata', I will go into this in more detail.

Hook punch and uppercut are both in kata.

The boxing version of hook and uppercut

The Pavement Arena

In addition to the lead hand punch and reverse punch that karate had already introduced me to, boxing offered the lead hand hook and uppercut, the reverse hand hook and uppercut, all of which could be used at short, medium or long range.

I was also encouraged to merge the punches together, forming bastardisations that could be aimed into small openings in an opponent's defences where the conventional straight, hook or uppercut punch found no entrance. This was the most exiting revelation. Boxing offered the experienced practitioner a limitless choice of punches, almost every punch thrown was slightly different from the last and no target was impenetrable. A straight right cross might not find its way through a tight guard, but, if you added a slight hook to it, the guard could be bypassed.

Punches in the dojo are nearly always practised at full extension, with control, thrust at the end and supported by the retracted opposite hand (hikatae).

Practising the punch at full extension develops power, when working with a partner it teaches correct distancing and control, and thrusting at the end of the punch promotes kime (body focus), which is essential again, for power. Retraction of the supporting hand to the opposite hip is instrumental in the transference of body-weight behind the punch. All these practices are important when learning techniques, they provide the foundation that all karateka need, the crawl before the walk before the run. Their body-building properties also help to forge the body into the fighting instrument that it must become if proficiency is to be established. This is not the only way to do it, most systems have their own core practices, but with karate these are the norm.

The dojo punch must be tailored for use in a street situation. After all you wouldn't wear a T-shirt and jeans to a wedding. As you change your clothes to fit the occasion so you should adapt your technique to suit the situation.

On the street the thrust at the end of your punch is neither necessary nor recommended. It will only slow your punch down and it is easy to focus without locking the punch. The punch should not be fully extended on contact with the target, rather try to punch several inches (up to a foot) through the target. This will ensure a full contact blow and also take into account any pull back from your opponent. What is good practice in the dojo could well serve to be your downfall outside. You may only get one shot, don't waste it.

Your mind is a little like a computer. Your training habits are like data being fed into it. If you only feed in controlled dojo techniques, then that is all you will be able to do when you are in a confrontational situation. While I agree that basic karate training is excellent I must also say that transition training is necessary if real fighting skills are your goal. If you want your response to a confrontational situation to be a full contact blow to the assailant, then it stands to reason that you must practise full contact blows. If you ask your computer for data that has not been fed into its memory bank, it will logically be unable to respond. If you want to get relevant data out, you need to feed a little in.

There is no need to retract the supporting hand when you throw a real punch. Remember it's just a part of the beginner's foundation. Eventually one must discard such supports and fight unaided. When you punch learn to transfer your body-weight without retracting your other arm as it is far better employed by your chin as a guard. When you throw your chosen punch do so from a 'natural fence' position rather than from the traditional 'on guard' stance. In a live situation adopting a fighting stance before striking will only serve to warn your assailant of your intentions, thus losing you the advantage of a pre-emptive strike should you wish to use it.

Your initial attack will be from a 'natural fence' position

Be a head-hunter, more specifically go for the jaw. Body shots do not work consistently on the street. The jaw is the ultimate target as a sharp, accurate shot to the jaw of an adversary will more often than not induce unconsciousness.

Always try to precede your punch or attack with some kind of brain-engaging question or statement even if it's just 'Why are you picking on me?' Speaking before you attack will engage the antagonists brain for the split second that it takes to launch your punch, maximising its impact and heightening the possibility of a knock-out. A punch that is not expected is far more likely to cause unconsciousness in an adversary as it cannot be prepared for, thus maximum shaking of the brain occurs. Back in the dojo, it is of course unreasonable to expect anyone to let you practise full contact punches on their face or jaw, however you can don the boxing gloves and practise heavy sparring.

The Pavement Arena

Alternatively, rehearse full contact blows on punch bags, pads, or strike shields. Vary the angle of the punches as much as possible to ensure that you cover all situations. Throw the punches from a 'natural fence' position and try to imagine that you are facing a real opponent, that perhaps your life depends on the strikes. Be sure to put your weight behind every punch.

Chapter Five

Blocks

Blocking movements take up a very big part of karate training, as well as martial arts training in general. Almost every defence demonstration you see in martial arts begins with the blocking of an attack, yet in street scenarios blocks are almost never utilised. When it kicks off outside the chip-shop nobody blocks, even if they have been trained to do so. Why do people spend so much of their time practising for something that they are never likely to do? The best means of defence in a real fight is attack. Blocks don't work. I have more questions about this one subject that anything else.

'Do blocks work?' I am asked.

'No they don't.'

You may see this as an exaggeration on my part but believe me it's not. I have witnessed thousands of street fights, and have been personally involved in hundreds. All, with rare exceptions, were exchanges of attacks.

The Pavement Arena

The fighters in these bouts covered a wide spectrum of fighting styles, boxers, karateka, grapplers, brawlers, judoka, aikidoka and street fighters, yet the only blocking techniques that I ever witnessed were by those unwilling or unable to fight who blocked blows with their faces.

It sounds sacrilegious but traditional blocks don't work in self-defence scenarios. These situations are so frenzied and the attacks so numerous that there is only time for ferocious attack and counter-attack.

In a fair fight where you meet an opponent on the common to settle your differences like gentlemen, you may find room for the odd block or parry, but even then attacks would predominate.

Most blocks are designed to stop straight punches. In the dojo where straight is great and we all comply with the rules they do work admirably. For these reasons I still advise conscientious practise of blocks. Even if you only ever use blocking techniques successfully once in a lifetime, it will have been worth it.

Paradoxically many blocking techniques do find favour when used as attacks. A rising block can be effectively used as a forearm smash or even as a choke (see illustration). Outside-inside blocks can successfully double as hammer-fist strikes (see illustration). Knife-hand blocks can be effectively employed as chops – no not pork chops. Downward blocks again make good hammer-first strikes (see illustration). Inside-outside blocks act nicely as inverted back-fist strikes.

Knife-hand block

Knife-hand block and its application

Downward block

Downward block and its attack application

Rising block . . .

The Pavement Arena

. . . and its applications

Chapter Six

Kata

Throughout this chapter the term 'kata' includes 'forms', 'sets' and 'patterns'.

What are kata? My wife Sharon gave the best answer to this question when she said that 'Kata are whatever you want them to be.'

To the fitness orientated kata build stamina, strength, speed and power. They also enhance suppleness and balance. To the technician they tender the ultimate challenge, demanding a combination of timing, balance, footwork, distancing, kime, attitude and still more. A challenge that can and does last a lifetime.

To the practitioner who wishes to go beyond physical technique and into the labyrinths of mind training, kata are a series of mentally challenging exercises that can forge a strong and indomitable spirit.

The Pavement Arena

Last though not least, for the karateka wishing to pursue knowledge of self-defence kata are a treasure trove of hidden techniques that can be adapted directly to a street situation. For more on kata applications see Iain Abernethy's marvellous book 'Karate's Grappling Methods' and his videos. All of the skills developed by kata are necessary when street defence is called for.

While kata themselves may not be directly relevant to the street, indirectly they certainly are. It's a matter of perspective – if you want to see them as unrealistic and impractical you will. If however you are perceptive enough to see, you will find that they offer enormous benefits to the street-orientated.

To the practitioner who wishes to use kata as a means of developing their mental powers, I advise that they learn the correct bunkai of each technique within their chosen kata. Visualising kata entails using the techniques on imaginary opponents. If you do not know what the moves mean or represent this becomes an impossible task.

Many of the moves have more than one application. Try to find one which suits you, then visualise it when you practise. My own kata search brought me much enlightenment as it showed me that karate lacks very little if viewed from the correct perspective.

It is not the content of the karate syllabus that is lacking, more that the syllabus is not fully utilised. A closer look at kata will divulge not only the manoeuvres we have all come to know and love, but also grappling movements, throws, hook and uppercut punches, eye gouges, grabs, knee attacks, ankle stamps, joint strikes, head-butting and even ground fighting techniques. Have a look at your own dojo. How much of this vault of information has been discovered, utilised and taught therein?

When I had my own karate club all these techniques and more were covered. Why? Because they encompass every eventuality in all scenarios, a necessity if one is to be at all prepared for an attack.

The pavement arena does not suffer fools gladly. Once you are familiar and competent with the bunkai, use visualisation to put them into practice. When you strike, imagine your opponent, their grimacing face, aggressive gait and the effect that your strike has on them. If you have experienced violence in a real situation, use the experience to enhance your visualisation practice. Picture your blocking technique fracturing your opponent's arm or leg, your strike knocking them unconscious, their body plummeting to the floor.

Undoubtedly you will at first experience difficulty in retaining these images. Throughout the kata, your mind, unused to strong and prolonged concentration, will drift off with annoying regularity. With practise you will gain greater focus and quickly bring to attention any drifting moments. Eventually your mind will grow in strength, even spilling over into the rest of your life, greatly heightening your survival chances. A strong mind is of fundamental importance when controlling a violent confrontation.

Although kata vary from style to style and from system to system, one thing remains universal. All have hidden bunkai. Search, ask, learn and practise. Here is a selection of techniques from Shotokan kata.

Kata movement

Application

Kata movements

Applications

Kata movements

Applications

Kata movements

Choke application

These are just a few examples of the hundreds of bunkai found within kata, just waiting to be discovered and applied.

Chapter Seven

Set Sparring

Most systems of karate have some form of set sparring on their syllabus. Two opponents pair off to practise preset attacks and defences. It may be five-step, three-step, one-step or semi-free sparring. Again the uninitiated tell us that these movements and practices are too far detached from reality to be of any real use. This would be true if the movements were meant to pertain to real fighting, but they are not. They are, in fact, just a small part of the apprenticeship that a karateka has to undertake before transition to realism can occur. After all, a bricklayer has to learn how to lay mortar before he can build a wall and a pilot has to study aviation before he can fly a plane. So it is with karate. The basic movements, kata, set sparring, and so on are to the karateka what laying mortar is to the bricklayer and aviation is to the new pilot. Again, this is not the only way to build a foundation, indeed you might feel that it is not the best way, but we hopefully would all agree that it is the karate way.

Everything that we do in karate has a meaning or purpose. For this reason tradition should not necessarily be regarded as impractical or unrealistic, for while a particular movement may be both, the fruit of the conscientious practice of the same technique can be amazing.

I have to tell you right now that I no longer practise or teach the basics in the karate way. I have found a better method for my students and me. I am not saying that it is a better way for every one, as preferences in martial arts are very subjective, but it suits us. If you practise Shotokan it is probably because the Japanese style suits you as a person, if you like wing chun, perhaps the Chinese system is more to your taste. I only found a new way by exhausting the old. The purpose of this book is to try and enlighten those who choose the karate way, to show them the meaning of the movements they make.

The greatest benefit derived from preset sparring is that it teaches correct distancing, as well as control, timing and to a lesser degree, footwork. If practised correctly it also helps with fear control.

The Pavement Arena

Correct distancing is fundamental to any fighting system, outside or inside the dojo, and it is imperative if success is to be attained in a confrontational situation. Distancing becomes instinctive through the regular practice of set sparring. If you don't practise it how will you know when the distance is correct to launch an attack? Is the opponent too close or too far away? How do you correct that distance if it is wrong?

In most of the street fights I have witnessed where the fighters were inexperienced, 90 per cent of the blows missed their target because the attackers had no conception of distancing. Set partner work programmes drill correct distancing into your fighting brain and you can immediately recall it should the necessity arise. You learn to feel when the distance is right or wrong, moving backwards if you are too close, forwards if you are too far away.

One-step sparring. Defender in ready stance.
Attacker prepared to attack the stomach.

Attacker steps forward with a stomach punch. Defender steps back and blocks with an outside-inside block.

Defender counter-attacks with a reverse punch to the jaw, using kiai (spirit shout).

Set partner work is also excellent for acquiring controlled technique, teaching you to pull your attack on impact with the opponent, allowing hours of uninjured practice. However it has its limitations. At some point you have to ditch the semi-contact practice because it develops a negative muscle memory. If you train to pull your blows then the chances are when you get into a real affray that is exactly what you will do. At some point you will need to transfer your skills to the punch bag or training pads so that you can practise full contact blows. Remember, you get what you train for.

Control doesn't just mean stopping on impact. Control comes in varying degrees, from touching the surface of the opponents skin to breaking the skin or ultimately, as a last resort, striking with a full contact blow.

The footwork learned in set practice is basic but still worthy of a mention. You need to learn how to move and strike or block simultaneously. Stationary punching and mobile punching are completely different. Loss of balance and mistiming will occur if moving simultaneously with a technique is not practised. Although the forward and backward steps taken in five- and three-step do not pertain to real situations, the more advanced ju-ippon kumite (semi-free sparring) does get a lot closer.

Think of five-step as the baby crawling, three-step as the baby walking with a frame, one-step, the baby toddling, semi-free sparring, the baby walking with confidence and all out sparring, the baby running. You have to learn to walk before you can run.

If you wish to practise fear control whilst working in set partner scenarios, then you have to introduce fear into the syllabus. This is easily done. When it is your turn to attack try as hard as you can to hit your partner. This will immediately introduce realism into the practice, the ugly handmaiden of realism of course being fear. If your partner really believes that you are trying to hit them, it will fill him or her with a mixture of fear, apprehension and confusion – 'Don't they know that they're not supposed to hit me?' The fact that fear has been forced upon them will compel them to handle it. Fear control. All of a sudden dull set partner work becomes terrifyingly real, invoking all of those horrible feelings that we hate so much.

All of these manufactured feelings are the ones that we need to feel and get used to if character development is to occur.

These feelings, triggered by adrenaline, are the same that occur when we are attacked, in many cases causing the infamous 'freeze' syndrome that can stop you faster than cyanide tea. Many people in the dojo run from these feelings, avoiding partners who cause them. These runners will not survive in the pavement arena. If they can't handle these feelings in a controlled environment they have little chance of doing so when it's for real.

To develop as a karateka and desensitise yourself to fear, you must confront these feelings again and again until you no longer fear them. Seek out aggressive partners who lace their attacks with real intent.

If you find yourself partnered with the club pacifist – there are loads in every club – make sure when you attack that you try to hit them. You will find that once you attack with malice then your partner will reciprocate, even if it's only to get their own back on you.

The Pavement Arena

As well as instilling fear into set partner work this method of practice also has another bonus as it shows you the effectiveness – or ineffectiveness – of your attacks and defences. If you do not attack hard enough you will not get through their defences, if you do not block strongly you'll get hit. Many people practise set partner work without any realism. When they attack they aim to miss, sometimes subconsciously, aiming above, to the side, or short of the target, with no real intention of hitting the opponent, even if he or she fails to block. This person is best avoided. Always look for an opponent who you know will hit you if you are not on the ball, the person everyone usually avoids.

To strike the face initially I recommend the use of control. I consider a cut lip good control. To attack the body strike hard, adjusting your control according to the standard of your partner.

At first you may find this a little hard, even unreasonable, but if you do not practise this way you are wasting your own time and your partners. You'd be better off sitting down and watching.

As a concluding point, do not look upon a partner as male or female. Don't treat the ladies with kid-gloves, this is the height of disrespect. A woman in the dojo should be treated as an equal in all respects. To do any less would be to send her out into the world ill-prepared and perhaps to her doom. Woman need to be shown reality more readily than men because unfortunately they are victimised far more.

Chapter Eight

Free Sparring

This is the final part of the jigsaw. Some place great emphasis upon it, others avoid it like the plague. In all honesty if you don't spar the learning process is greatly impeded, in fact you will struggle to get past basic technique. In metaphoric terms, if basic technique is the bricklayer laying mortar, then sparring is his transition to actually building a wall. Free sparring is where everything should come together, where you try out and practise new techniques against opponents who are doing their utmost to stop you while trying out new techniques themselves. It is the final step before matriculation to the street.

Because of the unrealistic way most people practise free sparring, that step is often a very large one and when it is taken disorientation occurs. Most karate dojo practise karate sparring or contest sparring, and whilst this can be enjoyable and very skilful it is not real. Even when the fighters pick up the pace and use less control it is still not real. Legs fence legs, and punches, predominantly straight, will be eagerly exchanged. Occasionally a cut lip will emerge from the exchanges, even a winding, and the fighters will think 'Yes, this is real'. But it isn't. It may be real for the dojo, even the contest arena, but sadly, for the street it is greatly lacking.

It matters not that your kick was fast or that your punches were powerful because you, your partner and your joint techniques are all within the confines of set rules. Contest rules, dojo rules, or unspoken rules of conduct.

If you exchange blows with an opponent in the street and your bodies clash, will you mutually break the embrace and continue the fight at kicking or punching range?

Will 90 per cent of your hand techniques be aimed at the body?

In the dojo will your partner butt, bite or choke you if you get too close?

In the street will your opponent let you wipe your nose if it's bloody?

The Pavement Arena

Let you rest if you feel a little tired?

Take it easy on you if you feel 'hung over' from the night before?

When he attacks you, will he deliberately aim to miss you?

Think closely about a real situation. How near to that are you when you spar? The first step to realistic sparring is to discard most of the rules. Try progressive sparring.

In progressive sparring anything goes. You could initiate the fight with a roundhouse kick to the face and culminate the fight with a submission choke on the floor. If you throw a lazy kick and your opponent catches your leg, you'll be wrestling until one of you submits. An opponent who is being out-kicked or out-punched may seek the sanctuary of grappling range where he can butt, bite and choke. If you can't grapple in this situation you'll certainly lose every time.

Progressive sparring forces the kicker to retract his kicks quickly and also to be choosy about when and where he kicks. The puncher will also be forced to be very sharp with his punches and light on his feet if he is to avoid the grappler. The non-grappler will learn to grapple out of necessity.

Remember, a puncher will always beat a kicker and a grappler will always beat a puncher. Remedy? Learn to kick, punch and grapple. A chain is only as strong as its weakest link. Find your weakest link and strengthen it with extra knowledge and practice.

My weakest links, many years ago, were punching and grappling. To strengthen them I joined a judo club and a western boxing club. Practise restricted sparring to strengthen you weak areas. Here are a few ideas.

When I talk about the importance of progressive sparring it isn't to say that it is the be-all and end-all. Other forms may and should be practised as too much heavy sparring can be detrimental to the learning process. Sometimes you have to play, after all, no-one is going to try out new techniques if they think that they're going to get trounced every time they make a mistake.

The Pavement Arena

Using semi- or no contact blows can allow both parties to practise and develop new techniques happy in the knowledge that if they do make a mistake they are not going to be heavily penalised for it.

Heavy progressive sparring though should be a regular part of your training regime. It is the forge training, where blades are tempered and spirits forged. As I stated earlier, in this genre of sparring anything goes. To stop major injuries you have to make sure that it is done under some kind of supervision. Use control at all times when biting or butting for obvious reasons. When employing a biting technique it is enough to nip and then release. There is no need to produce a severed ear to validate the bite. If the opening arises the butt should be employed. Again a tap is enough to let the opponent know that you were there. If the fighting spills over into grappling, it is not advisable to throw an opponent without the cushion of mats or knowledge of break-falls.

Ground fighting is again, all out. Always practise the tap system for submissions from chokes and locks. Tap yourself, your partner or the floor should you wish to submit or give in. Never continue a hold after the opponent has tapped, release immediately. It is also very dangerous to employ choking techniques without the supervision of an experienced instructor. If your opponent's arms are tied up and their mouth covered, they may not be able to tap or signify submission which could quite easily end in a fatality.

Summary

Practise all kinds of sparring, especially heavy progressive, which is undoubtedly the closest you will get to the real thing. Wear protective gloves and headgear for extra safety.

Chapter Nine

Competition Fighting: Friend or Foe

By Ian McCranor 6th Dan
Former Commonwealth Silver Medallist

I've called this chapter 'Friend or Foe' because that is how I see the difference between fighting a competitor in a tournament and an aggressor in the street.

When you train for competition everything is geared to what the referee wants to see, what scores a point. You work hard on your control and fast pull back, quick movement and fast footwork. Feints and sharp stance changes are all part of a competition fighter's rigorous training.

The competition fighter knows that he or she is fighting a friend. The bow at the beginning signifies this and although not a word is spoken both fighters know that no matter how rough it gets out there, there will be a handshake at the end of the bell.

The word 'hajime' signals the start of the bout and 'yame' can be called at any time to stop the bout. A buzzer gives both fighters notice that the fight is drawing to an end, so that the fighters can then act accordingly.

The techniques most widely used in WUKO (World Union of Karate-do Organisations) are ones that, it is fair to say, inflict the least damage. Reverse punches to the body are the most commonly used punches, followed closely by front punches and uraken (back-fist strikes).

The most commonly used kicking techniques are roundhouse and reverse roundhouse kicks. Add a few clever sweeping techniques and then combine all of the above and you have WUKO competition.

I am, I must say, a great lover of the WUKO system and think the rules as they stand are fine. I also think that people who knock point-scoring have absolutely no idea of the fitness levels required, the accuracy of technique needed or the timing and sheer skill involved. WUKO at top level promotes some of the world's finest athletes.

The Pavement Arena

I am presently, and have always been, heavily involved in the WUKO system.

I teach karate and competition karate professionally. I also, however, work on a pub door as a bouncer. When the fighting starts here I am no longer dealing with friends in a competition arena, I am dealing with foe. There is no 'hajime' or 'yame', there is no buzzer to let me know that the bout is soon to end, there is rarely a handshake and never a trophy for the winner.

The butterflies in your stomach before you fight a friend turn into alligators when confronted by a foe. I have dealt with both friend and foe, and my club teaching reflects this. These fights are different but good competitors will have no problem making the necessary changes to their techniques.

You have to make your techniques deliberately hurt to stop the opponent dead in their tracks. In a competition if you draw blood or your contact is too heavy, then you are looking at a warning or disqualification. No-one who wants to win a tournament is going to deliberately break his opponent's nose or crack his ribs, so it is fair to say that when this kind of thing happens it is accidental. Only when you can stop your opponent at will, time and time again, will you know that you have the skill and the tools to deal with foe.

Epilogue

So, there it is! That's how I see it. Not a comprehensive book, not the biggest text in the world, it probably only took you a few hours to get through it. But if you are perceptive enough to take in all the information on offer, this baby might one day save your life. It has mine.

I admit that as a writer I am in the business of trying to make a living via this and other books, but if doing so meant telling fibs or clouding issues then without doubt I'd be back on the building site laying bricks, and not very well either. My morals are very high and I'm not in the habit of telling lies to make money. The changes that I promote within this text are the exact changes that I made to my own syllabus when many years ago I began my colourful career as a nightclub doorman. For this reason, and this alone, I can categorically state that the way I paint it is the way it is, no more no less. It is not how I think it is, or even how I think you would like it to be, it is simply how it is.

Adhere to the prescribed techniques of change, addition and subtraction and you will become enlightened, strengthened both mentally and physically, and above all prepared!

You don't need to discard karate for another martial art. Everything has a meaning or purpose though sometimes you may have to dig a little to find it.

'The iron ore feels itself needlessly tortured in the furnace, but the tempered blade looks back and knows better.'

– Traditional Japanese Proverb

Thank you for reading.

God bless

Geoff Thompson 2001

THE ELEPHANT AND THE TWIG

The Art Of
Positive Thinking

14 Golden Rules to Success and Happiness

GEOFF THOMPSON

author of *Watch My Back* and *Fear*

SUMMERSDALE

GEOFF THOMPSON

WATCH MY BACK

'I train for the first shot – it's all I need.'

'LENNIE MCLEAN HAD THE BRAWN, DAVE COURTNEY HAD THE CHARM, BUT GEOFF THOMPSON IS IN A CLASS OF HIS OWN.' FHM

www.geoffthompson.com

www.summersdale.com